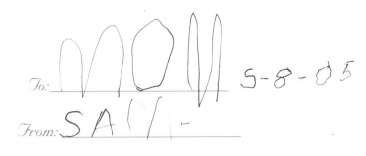

To: MOM   5-8-05

From: SAM

May the LORD *repay you for what you have done. May you be richly rewarded by the* LORD.

Ruth 2:12

Project & Design Manager: Amy E. Langeler
Associate Editor: Molly Detweiler
Design: Sherri L. Hoffman
Printed in China

01 02 03 04 /HK/ 8 7 6 5 4 3 2 1

Mom, You've Blessed my Heart

Written and Illustrated by

Audrey Jeanne Roberts

inspirio

The gift group of Zondervan

Dear Reader,

If you are receiving this book as a gift from your child, I hope that you can read each story and tribute and hear your own child's heart reflected in them. Perhaps your child has bought you this book because he or she deeply desires to honor your love, commitment, and mothering skills but like most of us feels inadequate to express those feelings in words.

The gift of mothering is one of the most fruitful, yet least recognized, gifts in our world today. If children succeed in life, it is often because of the love, encouragement, and prayers their mother invested in them. Each mother labors in a hidden place, away from the limelight, seeking to build her children up and make them secure in her love before she sends them out as ambassadors to a greater world.

The stories, poetry, reflections, and tributes shared here are only a tiny portion of the honor due to you as a mother. The value of your faithfulness, day in and day out will only be fully known when you enter the kingdom of heaven and hear, "Well done good and faithful servant! You have been faithful with a few things; I will put you in charge of many things. Come and share your master's happiness!" (Matthew 25:21). My heart's desire is that this little book will give you a moment of rest and reward this very day.

Sincerely,

Audrey Jeanne Roberts

Audrey Jeanne Roberts
Oak Haven Orchards
Valley Center, California

$\mathcal{M}$y thanks to the mothers in my life:
Thank you Mom, Carolyn Rogers, for giving me both physical and spiritual life—you gave me the greatest gift of all when you helped me place my trust in our Lord Jesus.

To my stepmother, Elizabeth, though I was a mother myself when you entered my life, you have encouraged me and shared in the joy of my accomplishments as though I were your very own.

Many thanks to my mother-in-law, Charlotte Brennan, who gave me her love and acceptance when I wed her son Jim and shared my deep sorrow when we lost him much too soon.

To my mother-in-law, Elizabeth Roberts, who has never had a single discouraging word for me—your complete acceptance and delight in me as a daughter has brought me great joy.

Much love and thanks to my grandmothers, "Nanny" Mary Louise Heyser who went home to be with the Lord in 1990. She loved to spoil me rotten—then send me home for my mother to straighten out! Thanks also to my Grandma Elaine Flint who prayed for me faithfully in the twelve years we were apart and who has blessed me richly in the years we've been restored.

To my spiritual mothers (too many to name!) who have loved me as I was, but loved me too much to let me comfortably remain there. You have challenged me to grow in Christ until he is fully formed in me.

And most of all, thank you Lord for allowing me the great privilege and joy of becoming a mother myself—and for giving me the strength and resources equal to the enormity of the task!

Every good and perfect gift is from above.
James 1:17

Table of Contents

You loved me enough to teach me right from wrong . . .

You loved me enough to lead me to my Heavenly Father.

You knew I needed to be capable of doing things for myself . . .

Thank you, Mom, for all you've done to give me life and for teaching me how to live it! I love you.

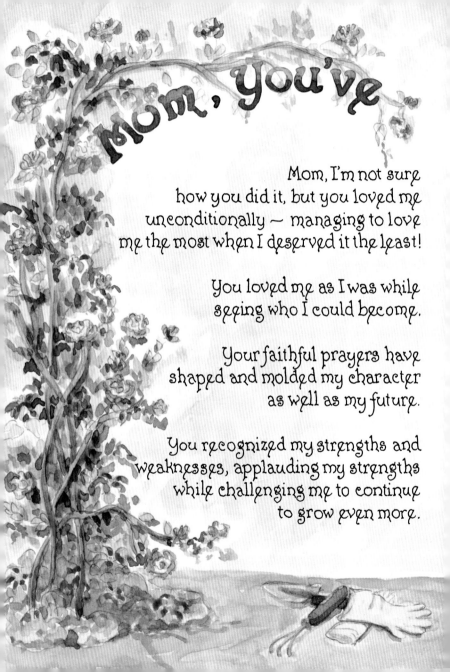

Mom, you've

Mom, I'm not sure
how you did it, but you loved me
unconditionally ~ managing to love
me the most when I deserved it the least!

You loved me as I was while
seeing who I could become.

Your faithful prayers have
shaped and molded my character
as well as my future.

You recognized my strengths and
weaknesses, applauding my strengths
while challenging me to continue
to grow even more.

Blessed my Heart

You built me up where I was weak.
You encouraged me when I was
frustrated and downhearted. At times
It felt like you were the only one who
believed in me ~ even when I wasn't
capable of believing in myself.

As a child, I remember clearly how
one look from you could set me
straight! Then those same eyes
could gently affirm me, saying "You
can do it!" or "I believe in you" or
"You're my child. Remember
that I love you with my
whole heart."

One touch from you could heal my hurts,
from skinned knees to a bruised heart.
All I needed was your arms
wrapped around me for the world
to recede away. You helped me
feel contented, safe, and loved.

You attended to thousands
of mundane, repetitive tasks for
only one reason — you loved me.

You also loved me enough to teach
me right from wrong, to be neat,
and to care for those smaller
than myself. You loved me enough
to lead me to my Heavenly Father.

Right from the start, somehow
you knew that to be successful,
you had to work yourself

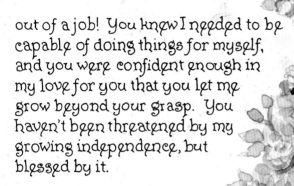

out of a job! You knew I needed to be capable of doing things for myself, and you were confident enough in my love for you that you let me grow beyond your grasp. You haven't been threatened by my growing independence, but blessed by it.

You were my first friend. You listened to my jokes ~ and even laughed at them no matter how silly they were. Now you are my best friend.

Thank you, Mom, for all you've done to give me life and for teaching me how to live it!

I love you.

The Seasons of a Mother's Life

One morning I lay in bed tempted to pull the covers over my head. I was dreading the thought that my Bible reading for the day was going to be Proverbs 31! My children were very small and each day I started with a to-do list that was never-ending. The myriad of repetitive tasks, like picking up toys, washing two loads of laundry every day, cooking, cleaning and comforting, consumed my time leaving no room for anything that felt "important" or could meet my need for significance.

My husband was supportive. He never minded if the house wasn't picked up because I'd chosen to spend the day at the park. He would remind me, "A special day with the girls is more important than a perfect house." In reality, it was my own internal expectations that made me feel guilty—I felt like I should be able to manage it all.

In light of all this, I was not prepared to read a chapter extolling the praises of a woman who not only handled all of these tasks with ease, but "considered a field and bought it," "selected wool and flax and worked them with her hands," much less one who "had servant girls to instruct!"

As my pity party was preparing to swing into high gear, the still small voice of the Lord insisted that I get out from under the covers, turn to this passage, and look at it with fresh eyes. His gently persistent voice sounded a question in my mind—"So Audrey, look closely and tell me, do you think she did all of these things in a single day?"

A new perspective was born in my heart that day.

Curiosity peaked, I grabbed my Bible and read the passage through several times. A new perspective on life was born in my heart that day. As a woman born and raised in the height of the feminist movement, I had always believed what I had been told: "You can have it all, *right now*!" Television shows made it seem easy to meet the needs of a family and have plenty of energy left over for a spectacular career, private time and even elegant entertaining. But when I tried to emulate this model, my life simply felt more and more out of control and overwhelming.

The Lord opened my eyes to see that he had set no limits on *what I could accomplish*. But for my life to be full and satisfying, he *had* designed it to be lived in seasons. The woman who was praised in Proverbs 31 accomplished her tasks over a long season of time—not in a single day!

What a wonderful sense of freedom that one realization brought to my heart. I felt the burden that came from trying to meet impossible expectations lift from my shoulders.

I realized that in that season of life a successful day was when I changed my baby's diapers, kept her clean and made sure she was safely corralled. Over the next few years, it would be more than enough for me to clean my house, play with my toddlers, and learn more about God's Word. Later in life there would be exciting and productive seasons when I would be called to teach, produce, accomplish, and lead. At that particular season, though, my children, home and family were the tools God was using to develop my character and nature so that I might become more like him.

I also noticed in Proverbs 31 that it was probably at the end of this woman's season of raising her family when her children rose up to call her blessed. They were probably clueless as to how much she was doing for them when they were young.

Every mom feels unappreciated at times.

Every mom feels unappreciated at times. Her work seems mundane, her chores never-ending. She often has to attend to the boring, routine things when she'd much rather do the things that make her feel more accomplished and effective, like pursuing her own interests and talents. Her children not only forget to "bless her," they usually gripe about the very things she does because she loves them so much!

But no matter which season you find yourself in as a mother—if you have done the little things

Your family will eventually "rise up and call you blessed."

with a loving heart, it is assured that your family will eventually "rise up to call you blessed." Buying you this little book is one of the ways they chose to communicate that they appreciate all the little things you have done to make them feel safe and secure, even though they often forget to tell you so!

The Proverbs 31 Mom
Through the Eyes of Today's Mom

Who can find a virtuous and capable wife and mother?
She's worth more than her weight in stock options!
Her husband and children can trust her for she greatly
   enriches their lives.
She's the keeper of the schedule. She does her best
   to make time for special family gatherings.
She feels like she's successful when her family
   is successful.
She's secure enough to let others shine.

She is resourceful. She looks at her family's life
   and determines what she can do to continually
   improve it.
She shops carefully, going to great distances to bring
   good food and great bargains home with her.
   She gets up early (whether she likes to or
      not!) preparing breakfast, directing
      traffic, making doctor's
      appointments, scheduling the
      repairman and the dog's
      shots . . .all before the coffee
      finishes brewing!

She's knowledgeable about business, real estate, agriculture, the stock market and retirement planning.

She takes what God has given to her and finds ways to multiply it so that her family is blessed, fed and kept in warm, comfortable clothing.

She's tireless. She's a hard worker and she knows how to direct her family so that the endless lists of tasks, chores, and obligations are accomplished smoothly and effectively.

She resolves disputes, trains in righteousness and tells today's best joke all while preparing dinner, doing the laundry and helping her kids with their homework!

She's an incredible bargain hunter and deal maker!

She's not only up at the crack of dawn, but she works late into the night when she needs to, especially if her family is in need.

She's generous with the poor and others in her life. She doesn't hoard the blessing that God has given her—she gives freely and with love and concern.

She's fearless about the future because she knows that God will care for those she loves and because she has been diligent to do her part as well.

She loves things of beauty. Her home is not only physically warm, she's worked to make it a place of emotional warmth and beauty as well.

She's learned how to fix things if they're broken, decorate them if they're plain and keep them organized so they can be found again when necessary.

She's beautiful—inside and out. She takes care of herself, not letting herself get worn down and frumpy.

She lets God's beauty shine from her heart and she makes herself as beautiful as she can be on the outside to honor him and her family.

Her children are known as wise and godly because of her influence in their lives.

Her children have become leaders in the land because of the leadership skills she has imparted to them in her home.

As if all of this isn't enough she's a business woman too, creating goods or services to sell to others, or advancing in her career to the glory of God!

She mentors others, modeling strength and dignity. Her character is a testimony to the power of God to transform a life.

When she speaks, her words are wise and filled with kindness. She's an effective manager, and she gives instructions without lording it over others.

She monitors the household finances carefully and
  avoids the pitfalls of debt and reckless spending.
  She doesn't have to worry about the consequences
  of laziness because of her diligent and self-
  controlled spirit.

Her children rise up and call her blessed.
Her husband praises her to anyone who will listen:
  "I have the most incredible wife in the world— there
  are many who are smart and capable, virtuous and
  kind, but she surpasses them all!"

She is a woman of great beauty and her beauty will
  never fade.
It will sparkle out of her eyes and flash in her smile all
  her days because the nature of God shines through
  her bringing him honor and herself reward.
She never has to speak of her own goodness because
  her deeds shout it so loudly.
Her life is rich, satisfying and rewarding.

Her children arise and call her blessed;

her husband also, and he praises her:
"Many women do noble things,
but you surpass them all."
Charm is deceptive, and beauty is fleeting;
but a woman who fears the LORD is
to be praised.
Give her the reward she has earned,
and let her works bring her praise
at the city gate.

Proverbs 31:28–31

The LORD your God has blessed you
in all the work of your hands.

Deuteronomy 2:7

The Lord will reward everyone for whatever good he does.

Ephesians 6:8

Jane-of-all-Trades

By Amy E. Langeler

Mom was taxi driver for my friends and me, shuttling us to our many activities—dancing, swimming, cheerleading, gymnastics, soccer, and softball. Mom and I would laugh each time I had to change my clothes in the car on the way to my next activity. She'd pick me up from school and I'd quickly change into my gymnastics outfit, after gymnastics, she'd pick me up and I'd quickly change into my dance leotard . . .

Mom was my cheerleader and coach. She was there at every swim meet. I can still remember hearing my mother call each time I'd pull my head out of the water, "Pull, Amy, Pull!" She'd always be there at the end of the lane to help me out of the water, wrap a towel around me and show me my ribbon.

A few years later, while in college, I brought my new friend Matt home to meet my family. After meeting him, my mom prayed that we would become much more than "just friends." Mom became my prayer warrior and matchmaker. I attribute my marriage to my mother's prayers.

For my wedding, Mom became my "fairy godmother," making the day even more special with her own unique touch—cutting lace from her own wedding dress to sew onto the ring bearer's pillow and using my baby bonnet as a part of my bridal bouquet.

Thanks, Mom, for making my life so full of special memories by filling so many roles. I hope to instill into my daughter what you've instilled in me and to be to her the "Jane-of-all-trades" that you were for me.

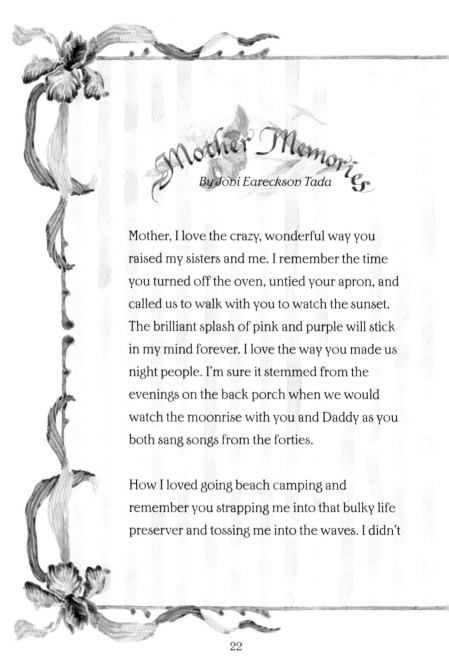

Mother Memories

By Joni Eareckson Tada

Mother, I love the crazy, wonderful way you raised my sisters and me. I remember the time you turned off the oven, untied your apron, and called us to walk with you to watch the sunset. The brilliant splash of pink and purple will stick in my mind forever. I love the way you made us night people. I'm sure it stemmed from the evenings on the back porch when we would watch the moonrise with you and Daddy as you both sang songs from the forties.

How I loved going beach camping and remember you strapping me into that bulky life preserver and tossing me into the waves. I didn't want to tell you how frightened I was of the gigantic swells. You hung on to my straps, and that was enough to chase the fear. Thank you for helping me to face fright head-on. Mother, do you recall watching Daddy hoist me into my new saddle on Thunder, that big Appaloosa? I cantered into the pasture, whooping and hollering. But I knew you were biting your nails, wondering if I could hang on. I love you for letting me be brave.

And thanks, Mom, for playing hopscotch with me. It seemed embarrassing that you, a grown woman, would toss an oak bark chip and jump around. But on the inside I was proud of you. Thank you for teaching me to appreciate older people. Thank you for teaching me about God. And table manners. For visiting me in the hospital nearly every day for more than a year after I broke my neck. What a mother.

We called my maternal grandmother "Nanny." By the
time I was born, no one in the family could remember how
or when the nickname started, but Mary Louise Heyser
reveled in it. Though she never made more than $1,000 a
month in her life, she showed me the incredibly precious
gift of giving.

Nanny had been a single mom. Her husband passed
away of a heart attack shortly after World War II, which
devastated her and left her with two young children to
support. At one time she worked three jobs just to keep a
roof over their heads and food on the table. She had no
college education, so she was limited to working physically
demanding jobs. She sorted avocados at a packinghouse.
She cooked for an elementary school and for Woolworth's
cafeteria. Eventually she secured a civil service job as a
secretary and finished her career serving our country.

Nanny lived simply. She saved carefully and rarely bought anything for herself. Yet she gave freely and abundantly to those she loved. When I look back now with adult eyes, I realize that she had very little, but as a child it seemed like she was very rich.

Nanny gave because she loved me.

I always sensed that Nanny didn't give to me to secure my love—she gave *because she loved me.*

My parents had a very limited budget. Most of our clothes were hand-sewn or hand-me-downs, so it was a treat for us to receive new clothing. Nanny loved to take my sister and me shopping for school clothes. She found great pleasure in the endless hours we spent trying on a multitude of new dresses and she traipsed from store to store as we meticulously picked out the prettiest socks, shoes, and hair bows to match.

We saw her generosity in both large and small ways. When my aunt and uncle got married, she gave them the house her late husband had built with his own hands because she wanted them to have a good start in life. She loaned money interest free to my parents when their car was totaled in an accident and they needed to buy a new one in a hurry.

She unexpectedly gave my husband and me two thousand dollars for the down payment and closing costs on our first condominium. As I stood open-mouthed and dumbfounded, with a twinkle in her eye she said, "I want to see you use your inheritance while I'm still alive to enjoy it!"

Nanny's generosity was the foundation upon which much of my life and career now rests. Our condominium appreciated quickly, and less than a year later we used the equity from its sale to purchase our first

"I want to see you use your inheritance while I'm still alive to enjoy it!"

home at a fixed and affordable rate, which enabled me to stay home with our children. The walls of that comfortable little "cottage" she helped provide for us also formed a cozy incubator from which my art career and business grew.

Nanny also gave me her time—investing herself in my life. She taught me to knit and crochet. She trained me in the fine art of embroidery and never once let my sloppy work on the back remain unchallenged! Through both genes and time in her home, she gave me a love for creating a beautiful home and things of beauty to bless others.

Nanny imparted her love for the garden deep within my soul, teaching me her simple wisdom for making things grow. Her city lot was completely covered with fruit trees and flowers, as she thought grass was an utterly useless waste of space. Nanny secretly delighted in watching school children sneak into her front yard and pick a flower for their teacher or for their mother. She would often come out and encourage them to cut even more rather than scolding them!

I wish I had recognized the greatness of Nanny's gift of giving when she was still with us. Yet in my heart of hearts, I know that she would have made light of what she gave had I expressed these thoughts to her and she would have been very uncomfortable receiving praise for something she would claim she did "for such selfish reasons!" I suppose the greatest thanks and tribute I could give her is to continue developing the gifts God has given me and to invest my time and talents in the generations that will follow in my footsteps, like I did in hers.

> *I wish I had recognized the greatness of Nanny's gift when she was still with us.*

I was young and now I am old,
*   yet I have never seen the righteous forsaken*
*   or their children begging bread.*
They are always generous and lend freely;
*   their children will be blessed.*

Psalm 37:25–26

A generous man will prosper.

Proverbs 11:25

Because of the service by which you have
proved yourselves, men will praise God for
the obedience that accompanies your confession
of the gospel of Christ, and for your generosity in
sharing with them and with everyone else.

2 Corinthians 9:13

Spiritual Mothers

I was 21 years old. Just two years earlier I had married and recommitted my life to the Lord at the same time. But marriage and life proved more difficult than I thought they would be and the pain and difficulty I was facing served to drive me to the Lord more and more intensively. At that time, I was led to a neighborhood "Women's Aglow" Bible study and I began to attend with a desire to learn all I could about the Lord and his ways. This group of women averaged ten to fifteen years older than me, and some were even old enough to be my mother.

Just a few months after I joined, the leader announced that the Lord was calling her to take a time of rest, and she was going to let go of teaching the study. Then she asked us each to pray about who among us was called to replace her. I faithfully prayed over the course of several days, envisioning each woman's face and asking God, "Is she the one you have called?" I had no sense of God's selection, so I continued praying.

One afternoon, the Lord unexpectedly broke into my thoughts. "Why haven't you asked me if I want you to

teach the Bible study?" My mouth dropped open in sheer astonishment! I had a hundred reasons why I wouldn't be the right choice, not the least of which being that I had never taught before in my life! I tried laying out my best arguments, "I'm too young. They would never have me.
I don't know enough." But as the next meeting approached, I kept sensing that the Lord wanted me to volunteer to teach.

Finally Tuesday afternoon arrived and I knew that I would be disobedient if I didn't share what I was feeling. So I snagged our leader on the sidewalk outside before she could go in. I started by saying, "I know this sounds crazy but . . ."

"I know this sounds crazy but..."

She laughed, looked toward heaven and said, "I've been telling the Lord all week he was crazy when he told me that you were to teach the study. Maybe we're both crazy! Let's go see what everyone else thinks."

The women in the study determined to seek God's answer about the question over the next week. The following Tuesday, I was unavoidably detained running errands and arrived an hour late. The women had been praying during that hour and had come to the conclusion that my leading was indeed God's will for our study. What I didn't know until fifteen years later was that they weren't particularly impressed with my knowledge or skill. Instead, the Lord had given them a picture that I was like a toddler

and they were to be a safe playpen for me! Their assign—
ment was to create a safe place for me to explore and grow.

The study used workbooks, so I thought it couldn't be
too hard to read ahead and guide the discussions. But the
workbooks didn't show up when they were promised. In
fact they didn't show up for months! Instead I had to decide
what to teach and then research it myself. I had to cry out
to God for his leading and be taught by him before I could
lead the others. In the next few years, God taught me much
more than those women ever learned from me!

Each of the women in the group knew so much more
than I, yet they had the grace to let me lead them. They
challenged me when I stretched the Scriptures too far.
They prayed faithfully for me and continually encouraged
me to keep teaching. When-
ever I had a need for prayer or
counsel, each in turn was used
of God to minister to my needs
and keep me walking the path
to maturity. When I think of

I marvel at their wonderful gift of spiritual mothering.

them today—Pat Faught, Sally Dotson, Char Iaquinta,
Debbie Pick, Midge Dow, Penny Dunn and many others—
I marvel at their teachable spirits and their wonderful gift
of spiritual mothering.

These spiritual mothers let me learn lessons on my
own, but hovered closely by to make certain I was safe.

They were there to counsel me when I needed it, but tried not to volunteer their advice until I asked for it. They prayed for me, sometimes praying soothing, comforting prayers, other times they silently prayed things I would never ask them to pray like "Lord, teach her patience. Refine her with your fire. Cleanse her from pride and sin."

My spiritual moms loved me enough to tell me when I was wrong.

My spiritual moms loved me enough to tell me when I was going in a wrong direction. They were proud of my growth and they invested time and energy in making sure I kept growing. They led me around the hidden land mines in life, sharing their own experiences along the way. Their gentle, gracious hearts prepared me to reach beyond myself.

Thank you Sally, Midge, Char, Penny, Debbie, Pat, and the many others along the way, for loving me enough to "mother" me! May these words also be a tribute to all "spiritual moms" and their priceless love for others.

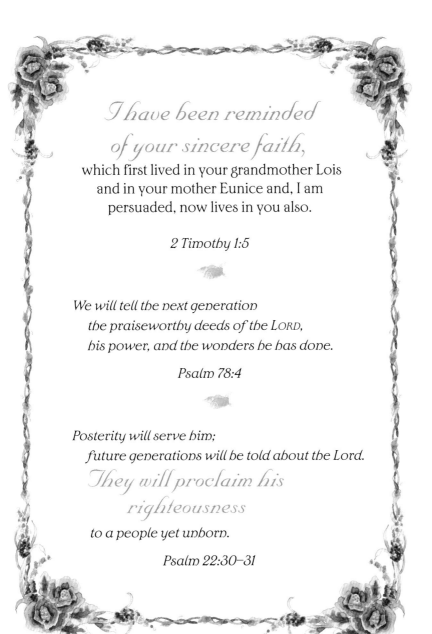

*I have been reminded
of your sincere faith,*
which first lived in your grandmother Lois
and in your mother Eunice and, I am
persuaded, now lives in you also.

2 Timothy 1:5

*We will tell the next generation
the praiseworthy deeds of the LORD,
his power, and the wonders he has done.*

Psalm 78:4

*Posterity will serve him;
future generations will be told about the Lord.*
*They will proclaim his
righteousness*
to a people yet unborn.

Psalm 22:30–31

The Mom Who Chose to Love

Most of us "mother" to the greatest degree during a short season of our lives—while our children are home. But for foster mothers, mothering full-time is a lifelong calling. Taking the most painfully abused and neglected children and loving them back to health and wholeness, these precious moms give their all to the task.

Sometimes their assignment is to help children that will eventually be restored to their natural families. In these cases they must be prepared to love deeply, yet release freely when the time comes. Other times they give their love to the unlovely, the rejected, and the forlorn. A foster mom's calling requires her to absorb anger and endure long periods of extreme behaviors and acting out until the children's hearts come to know that moms can truly be trusted. Gaining that trust is difficult. It isn't a predictable path. It requires tender sensitivity, a listening heart, and a constant crying out to God for wisdom and insight. Brandy's mom loved her like this, and God blessed that love by healing and restoring a lost child to wholeness— all through the gift of mothering.

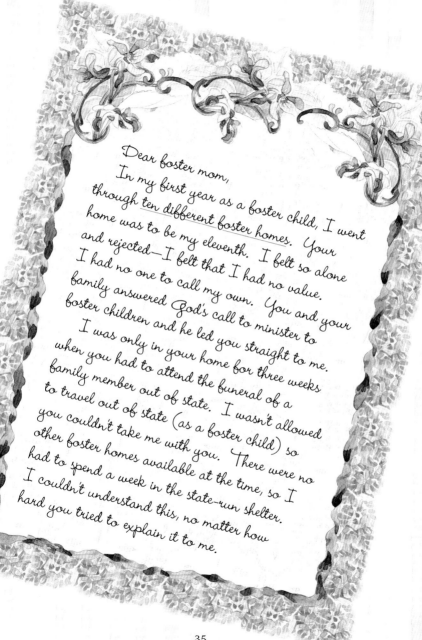

Dear foster mom,

In my first year as a foster child, I went through <u>ten different foster homes</u>. Your home was to be my eleventh. I felt so alone and rejected—I felt that I had no value. I had no one to call my own. You and your family answered God's call to minister to foster children and he led you straight to me.

I was only in your home for three weeks when you had to attend the funeral of a family member out of state. I wasn't allowed to travel out of state (as a foster child) so you couldn't take me with you. There were no other foster homes available at the time, so I had to spend a week in the state-run shelter. I couldn't understand this, no matter how hard you tried to explain it to me.

It seemed that nothing could break through to my fractured heart, for I was convinced that you were rejecting me, too. My heart was breaking and I was terrified. Finally I couldn't hold my question inside any longer. I blurted out, "What did I do wrong?"

Your soothing, loving response was, "You didn't do anything, Honey, this is just for a week until we get back from the funeral." But I'd been there before, I'd been reassured before— and in the end, I was always left alone again.

"No," I said, "You won't come back . . . they never come back." Each time I was left alone or shuffled from home to home it was a confirmation to my tender heart that I was worthless. Why would anyone ever want to come back for me?

You later told me how you paused and sought God's help asking, "How can I reassure her? How can I prove my love and commitment to her in a way she can believe and hold on to during the week we're going to be away? She needs desperately to know that she's loved and that there will finally be stability in her life."

You looked me in the eyes, tears brimming in your own, and reached down to your left hand. You took off your wedding ring, gently reaching for my trembling hand. "Here, I want you to keep this for me until I get back," you said, closing my fingers around the most tangible symbol of love and commitment that I could imagine.

From that moment forward, my life was forever changed. You did return for me. You continued to love me, and you slowly proved to me that I was indeed worthy of being part of our family. Mom, my life was forever changed by your incredible self-sacrificing love.

Thank you from the depths of my heart,

Brandy

My Other Mom

You have always been
there for me,
caring enough to teach me
and share your wisdom
with me,
but most of all
you have loved me
just like a mother.

I love you so much!

One look from you could set me straight . . .

or gently affirm me . . .

A Mother's Gentle Strength

Ada Lee Thurmon was the mother of one of my "spiritual mothers," Charlotte Iaquinta. I had the delightful privilege of being directly impacted by her wisdom in the course of my friendship with Char, as well as indirectly through Char's investing in my life.

The best way I can describe Ada Lee is that she was a living, breathing, walking, talking conviction! I never recall engaging in a conversation with her where I was not gently, but thoroughly convicted of my need to walk closer with our Lord and to let go of anything in my life that would hold me back from loving and serving him more fully. She had eyes that seemed to pierce through any pretense or mask and see directly to the issues of my heart.

Char often shared with me her mother's methods of raising her—and I quickly adopted them as my own in raising my girls! One story I particularly recall was of an evening when Char (normally a very obedient child) wanted to go to a party of which she knew her mother wouldn't approve. Her mother, sensing something either in Char's demeanor or simply by the "gift of discernment" God often gives mothers, realized that there was something amiss in this request.

Ada Lee was a wise woman. Rather than simply put her foot down, forbid Char's going and foster rebellion in her daughter's heart, she sent Char back to her room to seek the Lord's will in the matter. "If you sense not just Jesus' permission to attend, but also his pleasure in accompanying you to this party, then it will be all right with me as well."

Ada Lee was a wise woman.

What was Char to do? Lie to her mother? She already knew that the Lord wouldn't approve, and she knew that her mother *knew that the Lord wouldn't approve*—how was she to extricate herself from this mess? As Char thought through the predicament she was in, she slowly began to realize that her mother only wanted the best for her. Wisely, Ada Lee had chosen to entrust Char to the discipline of the Lord so that Char's own relationship with him would grow. You can imagine, however, just how hard Ada Lee must have been praying in the background while Char was wrestling with God in her room.

Eventually Char humbled herself before the Lord (and her mom) and took another step on the pathway toward maturity, all because her wise mother cared enough to confront her with the tough love of God.

In the early eighties I became caught up in watching the night-time soap opera "Dallas." But one gentle comment from Ada Lee was to transform the way I looked at entertainment and how it impacted my walk with God. She spoke not directly about my sin, but used a comment on what she had learned in her own life. "Whenever I catch myself rooting for people to sin," *Suddenly my eyes were opened.* she said, "I know that I have crossed a line with God and have entered into sin myself." Suddenly my eyes were opened and I realized that I was "rooting" for these TV characters to develop "love" relationships that were adulterous or based on lying, pretense, and lust. My viewing habits were challenged and changed for a lifetime in just a moment's casual conversation with Ada Lee.

Ada Lee was a strong woman, but she was a submitted woman both to the Lord and to her husband. She was a beautiful example of a woman eager to be used as much as the Lord desired, especially in meeting her responsibilities as a mother. Char was truly blessed to call her "Mom."

Our Mom

She never met a Bible she didn't love
or want to own.

She never met a person of any color
that she made a stranger.

Her shouted laughter shattered barriers
raised by others.

Her care for friends and family
wrapped them in warm beams of
summer's sun melting icy walls within.

Her prayers can still be heard—
softly ascending heaven's golden stairs
to God above who sent more answers than
we in our lifetimes deserve.

She'd be right there if anyone was going
for an ice cream sundae.

She'd beat you out the door to pay
a visit to God's house.

Our mom was big in body
and had a spirit larger than any one
person could seem to possess.

Her love abounded to all mankind
near at hand or Arctic far.

Her prayers were big enough to
wrap the world—
yet minute enough to cover
the twinkle in a child's eye.

She is our Mom.

Linda Fode

A Mother Who Wouldn't Give Up

by Dr. Ben Carson

I was perhaps the worst student you can imagine. In fact, my nickname was *Dummy*. I remember my midterm report card in [my fifth grade] class. I was doing so poorly I failed almost every subject.

My poor mother was mortified. Here she was, with a third-grade education, working two or three jobs at a time as a domestic, cleaning other people's houses, knowing that life didn't hold much for her, and seeing my brother and me going down the same road.

She didn't know what to do. So she prayed and asked God to give her wisdom. What could she do to get her young sons to understand the importance of education so that they could determine their own destinies?

God gave her the wisdom—though my brother and I didn't think it was all that wise. It was to turn off the television. From that point on she would let us watch our choice of only two or three television programs during the week. With all that spare time, we were to read two books a week from the Detroit Public Library and submit to her written book reports, which she couldn't read. But we didn't know that.

I was extraordinarily unhappy about this new arrangement. All my friends were outside, having a good time. I remember my mother's friend coming to her and saying, "You can't keep boys in the house reading. Boys are supposed to be outside playing and developing their muscles. When they grow up, they'll hate you. They will be sissies. You can't do that!"

Sometimes I would overhear this and I would say, "Listen to them, Mother." But she would never listen. We were going to have to read those books.

At any rate, I started reading. And the nice thing was my mother did not dictate what we had to read. I loved animals, so I read every animal book in the Detroit Public Library. And when I finished those, I went on to plants. When I finished those, I went on to rocks because we lived in a dilapidated section of the city near the railroad tracks. And what is there along railroad tracks, but rocks? I would collect little boxes of rocks and take them home and get out my geology book. I would study until I could name virtually every rock, tell how it was formed, and identify where it came from.

Months passed. One day the fifth grade science teacher walked in and held up a big shiny black rock. He asked, "Can anybody tell me what this is?"

Keep in mind that I never raised my hand. I never answered questions. So I waited for some of the smart kids to raise their hands. None of them did. So I waited for some of the dumb kids to raise their hands. When none of them did, I thought, *This is my big chance.* So I raised my hand . . . and everyone turned around to look.

They couldn't wait to see what was going to happen. And the teacher was shocked. He said, "Benjamin?"

I said, "Mr. Jaeck . . . that's obsidian." And there was silence in the room.

Finally the teacher broke the silence and said, "That's right! This is obsidian."

I suddenly realized that everyone was staring at me in amazement. But you know, I was perhaps the most amazed person in the room, because it dawned on me in that moment that I was no dummy. Within a year and a half, I went from the bottom of the class to the top of the class— much to the consternation of all those students who used to tease me and call me Dummy.

I pay tribute to my remarkable mother's influence almost every time I speak. And I have to agree with the countless people who approach me afterward to tell me, "You are fortunate to have a mother like that."

For My Single Mom

I watch you working much too hard,
and sometimes I don't make life any easier.
More than just a wonderful mom, you're a
counselor, cheerleader, taxi driver,
repairman... and more!
I want you to know
How much I love and respect you
and how proud of you I am.
Though life is often difficult
and it seems we don't have much,
it's the love that fills our home that
makes us feel so rich.
You're an incredible mother and
I thank God you're mine.

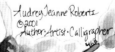

Audrey Jeanne Roberts
© 2001
Author · Artist · Calligrapher

47

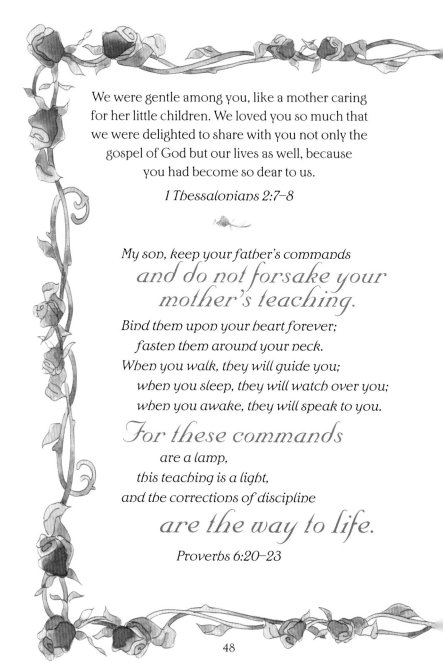

We were gentle among you, like a mother caring
for her little children. We loved you so much that
we were delighted to share with you not only the
gospel of God but our lives as well, because
you had become so dear to us.

1 Thessalonians 2:7–8

My son, keep your father's commands
and do not forsake your
mother's teaching.
Bind them upon your heart forever;
fasten them around your neck.
When you walk, they will guide you;
when you sleep, they will watch over you;
when you awake, they will speak to you.

For these commands
are a lamp,
this teaching is a light,
and the corrections of discipline
are the way to life.

Proverbs 6:20–23

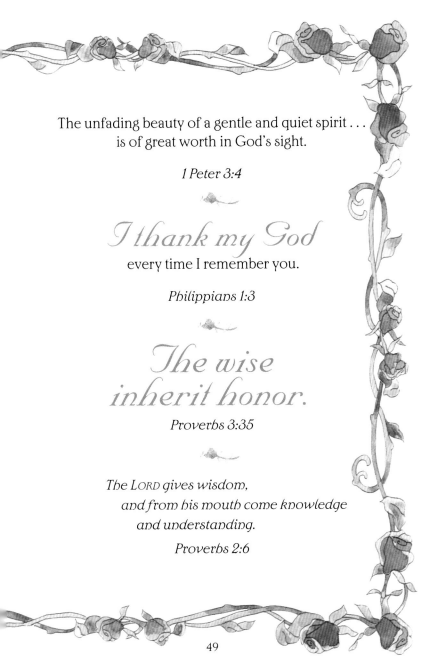

The unfading beauty of a gentle and quiet spirit . . .
is of great worth in God's sight.

1 Peter 3:4

I thank my God
every time I remember you.

Philippians 1:3

The wise
inherit honor.

Proverbs 3:35

*The LORD gives wisdom,
and from his mouth come knowledge
and understanding.*

Proverbs 2:6

Heirloom

Ann Weems
Retold by Alice Gray

It had belonged to Great-grandmother and he knew he must be very careful. The vase was one of Mother's dearest treasures. She had told him so.

The vase, placed high on the mantle, was out of the reach of little hands, but somehow he managed. He just wanted to see if the tiny little rosebud border went all around the back. He didn't realize that a boy's five-year-old hands are sometimes clumsy and not meant to hold delicate porcelain treasures. It shattered when it hit the floor, and he began to cry. That cry soon became a sobbing wail, growing louder and louder. From the kitchen his mother heard her son crying and she came running. Her footsteps hurried down the hall and came around the corner. She stopped then, looked at him, and saw what he had done.

Between his sobs, he could hardly speak the words, "I broke . . . the vase."

And then his mother gave him a gift.

With a look of relief, his mother said, "Oh thank heavens, I thought you were hurt!" And then she held him tenderly until his sobbing stopped.

She made it very clear—he was the treasure. Though now a grown man, it is a gift he still carries in his heart.

A Mother's Sacrifice

By Jessica Start

I was an eighth grader when asthma hit me for the first time—and it hit hard. That year I spent my birthday in the emergency room and the rest of the week in the hospital inside an oxygen tent. I was miserable and bored. I couldn't even watch television because condensation covered the inside of the plastic tent, leaving me isolated from the rest of the world by a cloudy mist.

During those long dull hours, my mother was always at my side, entertaining me, even playing cards long into the night when the medicine wouldn't allow me to sleep. She took such wonderful care of me.

I recovered at home for a full six months, unable to attend school due to a consistently low white blood count. My mother made the decision to quit her coursework at the University of Georgia to stay home and care for me. She put me first, and as a result of that decision she didn't return to school until many years later, graduating with her degree only a year or two ahead of me.

I don't think I realized the magnitude of Mom's sacrifice at the time. She willingly gave up her dream to care for me. I thank God for the wonderful mother he gave me and for the selfless heart he gave her.

A Mother's Heart

Is so tender
Filled with compassion for pain,
Patient with failures
While treasuring our gains...
Her love never ceases,
She's tireless it seems
Believing in our future and
Nurturing our dreams.
Whether laughing at mischief
Or possessing wisdom to impart.
She builds up her children
From the depths of her heart.

In view of God's mercy, ... offer your bodies
as living sacrifices, holy and pleasing to God—

*this is your spiritual act
of worship.*

Romans 12:1

Let us not become weary in doing good,
for at the proper time we will reap a harvest
if we do not give up.

Galatians 6:9

*He who refreshes others will
himself be refreshed.*

Proverbs 11:25

You loved me enough to teach me

right from wrong . . .

My First Teacher

Early in my parents' marriage, my mom began her college education with the goal of becoming a teacher. My arrival slightly altered her educational objectives . . . causing her to change from full-time to part-time attendance. Then she had my younger sister, Brenda, too. We were fortunate to become her "guinea pigs" as she practiced the tips and techniques she was learning in her classes on us. She was instrumental in our learning to read, teaching us phonics and spelling. Mom made learning such an integral part of our lives that our room décors prominently featured a blackboard where we could "play school."

Mom made learning such an integral part of our lives.

My mother took us to the library weekly and entered us in reading competitions there. When I wanted to quit the competition halfway through the summer, she wouldn't let me. She steadfastly encouraged us to complete the challenge and because of her diligence, I remember the satisfaction of achieving my first concrete goal. She helped me to read more than fifty books during the summer between kindergarten and first grade and then proudly displayed for all to see, the certificate the library gave us.

I must confess that we weren't always thrilled to have a teacher for a mom. Sometimes we thought it was very annoying. From our earliest days she taught us to speak in proper English, always utilizing proper sentence structure. She had the irritating habit of interrupting our excitedly told stories to correct our "I or me" usage. Often she would admonish us, "A woman who speaks well can be comfortable anywhere with anyone—even at the White House."

We weren't always thrilled to have a teacher for a mom.

One afternoon, many years later, I had the opportunity to lunch with a friend in the Congressional dining room in Washington D.C. In the middle of the conversation, my mother's instruction came back to my mind, and I laughed to myself, "You were right, Mom. Good manners and proper speech are important after all!"

My mother taught me more than head-knowledge. She also worked to instill a deep sense of right and wrong in my heart. One afternoon, I had stayed after class to help my third grade teacher. I lingered over a rock display one of my classmates had brought in. Deeply coveting a sparkling sandstone rock, I looked around to see if anyone was watching.

Then impulsively, before I had thought through the consequences, the rock found its way into my pocket and I quickly excused myself, leaving for home.

When I arrived home, I immediately went outside to play with the rock in my backyard. It shimmered dazzlingly in the sunlight, yet somehow my heart felt dark and heavy. I couldn't escape the nagging sense of having done wrong, no matter how I tried to silence the voice of my conscience. In my head I heard my mother's instructions, "Stealing is wrong. It hurts three people: the person that you steal from, yourself and most importantly it hurts God's heart."

My heart felt dark and heavy.

Within hours, my teacher called my home. She had either seen me take the rock or noticed it was gone and wanted to ask my mom about it. When mom found me, she didn't even have to ask the question. The evidence was sparkling in front of both of us. But she chose to let me come forward myself. "Audrey, is there something you've done that you need to confess to me and to the Lord?"

She led me through the process of repentance and forgiveness and then made me confess to my teacher and offer to make restitution in whatever manner the teacher felt was appropriate. The pain and sense of shame of that childhood act, wrote indelibly upon my heart the commandment "Thou shalt not steal!"

I was my mother's first student—but not her last. She was my first teacher, the one who prepared me to learn from other teachers. Her life continues to be spent investing in children. She taught school for many years. Now she volunteers at her local library, working with lonely latchkey kids who spend each afternoon there. Not only does she teach them to read and write and help them with their schoolwork, but she also invests her heart in loving them.

She invests her heart in loving.

This past week, I received a sleep-shattering call in the middle of the night. My mother had suffered a stroke. At only sixty-three she is now partially paralyzed and is working diligently to recover the use of her left side.

Our family traveled to visit her in the hospital. The day we arrived she had just been visited by one of the young boys she works with and his parents. He had made her a beautiful card by hand and had desperately wanted to go to the hospital so that he could bring it to her. It was placed pre-eminently, at the front of her nightstand along with a wondrous variety of cards made by many of her library and Sunday school students, and neighborhood children. She was overcome with emotion as she showed me one-by-one each card she had received from the children. The cards on her dresser attest to the power of a mother's love to change the world—one child at a time.

My Favorite Teacher, Mrs. Mom

By Molly C. Detweiler

My mother has always told me that she was born to be a mommy. She certainly had plenty of practice as the oldest of seven children. Her youngest brother was born when she was sixteen. "He was pretty much my baby," Mom said.

Mom's mothering skills continued to be put into good use during her first job after college, when she taught second grade at a rural elementary school. While she admits that she didn't really enjoy teaching school, she cherished the opportunities she had to mother her students. Many of them came from difficult homes where love and care were scarce, so Mom gave them her love at school.

During the school year she would take home two or three students at a time to spend the night at her apartment—a practice that would be unheard of today. This night was a highly anticipated event for the children, and many still remember it fondly to this day, even though they now have teenage children of their own! Mom would even buy new pajamas for some of the poorer studens and would spend the evening combing tangles out of their hair.

After three years of teaching, Mom decided that she wanted to be a mother for real and have a baby of her own. So she said goodbye to her students and said hello to me, her first baby. From experience I know that all that practice with little brothers and sisters and elementary kids paid off. She was a great mother—always willing to play with me, read to me, or just rock me to sleep. I remember loving my mom so much as a little girl that I thought I would burst. Every scrap piece of paper that I could find was covered with pictures and loving words for my mommy.

In my early elementary school years I began having a hard time going to school. I liked to learn and received good grades, but I hated leaving home. I was insecure and afraid much of the time. When I was in fourth grade and my brother was in kindergarten, my parents made the bold and difficult decision to home school us both. In the early 1980s home schooling was not widely accepted as an alternative to public school and my parents faced opposition from their own families about the decision. In spite of it all, Mom put her teacher hat back on and began doing lesson plans for a class of two.

The three years that I was home schooled were wonderful for me. I was able to learn at my own pace and be with my mom every day. Through my mother's gentle instruction I outgrew my insecurities and began to gain confidence. In eighth grade I returned to public school and enjoyed myself thoroughly, equipped with a newfound assurance of who God had created me to be, thanks to my mother's love. I am so thankful for the sacrifice of time and money that she and my father made to give me what I needed during those years.

Today, my mom's years of mothering her own children are done. We have both grown and begun our own lives. But her gift of mothering isn't going unused. She now works at her hometown library in the children's department. Once again she is befriending the children that others ignore—those with broken homes, dirty faces, and unruly behavior. She is paid very little for all that she does, but that's okay. What she does for those children is priceless.

My mother believes she was born to be a mommy. I and her countless "adopted children" thank God that she was right.

63

Mom, You Loved Me Enough

To teach me right from wrong
and challenge me to become
a person of faith & character.

You loved me enough
To live a life not perfect...
but worthy of imitation.

Through all the years,
in all you've said & done
I've always known

You loved me enough!

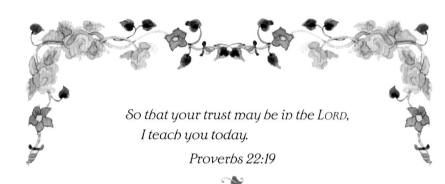

So that your trust may be in the LORD,
I teach you today.

Proverbs 22:19

The teaching of the wise
is a fountain of life.

Proverbs 13:14

Come, my children, listen to me;
I will teach you the fear of the LORD.

Psalm 34:11

Train a child in the way he
should go,
and when he is old he will not turn from it.

Proverbs 22:6

You loved me enough to lead me
to my Heavenly Father.

She Shepherds Her Lambs

Some of my earliest memories are of my mother teaching me about God. She made certain my sister and I attended Sunday school and Good News Bible studies as children. There weren't very many resources available to parents in her day, but she bought us the best books she could find. She even bought us an album of Bible stories called "The Wonderful World of Miracles" narrated by actor Walter Brennan.

My sister and I treasured that album. Like all children, we made her play it over and over and over again. She must have become tired of hearing it sometimes, but her enthusiasm never wavered as she continued to encourage us to sing along and memorize the Bible stories as we listened.

I remember accepting Christ as my Savior at Calvary Baptist Church in Placentia, California—probably somewhere between age three and four. My decision came from the fact that my mother continually led me to places where I could hear about Jesus and learn to love him. My mother was the instrument of not only giving me life, but leading me to the One who could give me life eternal.

Because my mother had been so diligent to teach me the Bible in my early years, by sixth grade I was longing for a deeper learning than I could receive in children's church. Mom was sensitive to my needs and asked if I could participate in her adult home group's Bible study. After some earnest discussion, Mr. Fusche, an elder in our church and the study leader agreed to allow her to bring me. With the practiced skill of a father of four, he patiently explained the verses we were reviewing in terms I could grasp and encouraged me to share my thoughts and insights (as childish as they were). Mom would often ask me questions during the week to help me remember what had been taught and would remind me to read that week's passage ahead of time so that I could be prepared for the discussion. She, and the other adults that attended, laid down their own needs, and suffered graciously week after week with my childish talkativeness, allowing me to learn a deeper love for God through their wisdom.

My mother led me to the One who could give me life eternal.

I rebelled strongly against my parents and the Lord in my late teen years, but it was the things that I learned in

Mr. Fusche's study about the book of Revelation that were instrumental in drawing me away from sin and back to the Lord. My mother's early diligence gave the Holy Spirit material to work with to convict me of sin and draw me back once again into fellowship with him. I discovered, like many other prodigal children, that there isn't any lasting "fun" in sin when there's a parent back home praying for your return. My mother saw the areas of my personality that could lead me into trouble. She saw the dangers ahead when I blithely raced into harm's way. She silently travailed at night when I was out with friends or on a date. While I gave her no room at the time for direct influence, I'm certain it was her cries that moved

The broken heart of a mother can be used by God to produce an abundant crop of righteousness.

God to protect me and ultimately bring me back to himself.

Later, during my step-daughter Ariane's own period of rebellion, I drew on my experience over and over again. It gave me the hope and confidence to entrust her to the Lord's hand, learning firsthand the same lesson my mother learned—the broken heart of a mother and her faithful tears can be used by God to produce an abundant crop of righteousness. Many a child—this one included—has made her way back to the Lord on a path made straight by her mother's prayers!

Mom, you were my first teacher and your lessons have formed the firm foundation upon which my life has stood, in spite of the storms raging about me. Thank you for all the skills and knowledge you took the time to teach me, but most of all thank you for teaching me about Jesus.

When I was growing up
I never realized that
you were such

A Special Mother

So many times
I took for granted your kindness,
I overlooked your sacrifices
on my behalf,
and barely noticed all the little
things you did to show you cared.

The wonder of it all
is that you loved me anyway!
You accepted me as
I was, and because you did,
I learned so much about
unconditional love.

Thank you for being such
a wonderful mother!

Treasure in a Jar of Clay

Mom, the physical strength of your jar of clay is
ebbing and you are slowly forgetting how to walk or even
drink soda from a can. You have Alzheimer's Disease
or "Old Timers" disease as your grandson called it years
ago when we first heard of your diagnosis.

I have watched you slipping away over the years —
perhaps it has only been ten — it seems so much longer.
First the driving skills faded, then your vocabulary and
ability to recognize most of your beloved twenty-four
grandchildren. Then you began to lose the intangibles like
your dignity, privacy and personal freedom. These things
are like large cracks in your vessel of clay. I can't tell
you how deeply I have wept for the mother you were and
over the mother you are now.

Yet, your spirit is not dying. Even in this late stage
of your disease, when I hand you a Bible, you will read
it out loud to me for hours on end. This amazes your

doctors, who usually see this skill disappear in the earliest stages of the disease.

You were always a prayer warrior and you still are today! If we ask you to pray with us, you pray virtually prophetically and with incredible power. When I am caring for you and begin to sing an old hymn you will finish the rest of the song. This has been such a testimony to me that when you fill yourself with the things of God, they will never fade away. The things of the Spirit are the things that endure.

Mom, you were such a godly mother. I watched you in my youth daily spending hours in prayer, worship and reading God's word. You loved each of your six children enough to lead us to him. Your life has been a testimony to faithfulness. You filled your heart with the things of God and they have remained there as eternal treasures. Though now there are large cracks in your clay jar, they are allowing God's holy light to shine through all the more.

I love you,

SallyLou

Mother's Pearls

By Char Iaquinta

Dear Mother,

Yesterday as I dressed for work, I chose to complete my outfit with your pearls. They reminded me of you and symbolized strength and courage when I felt over-whelmed with "busyness." As I fastened them, I realized that just as the luster of natural pearls lends a touch of elegance and understated style to clothing, "pearls of wisdom" gathered throughout life contribute even greater elegance and style to character. Though I treasure this string of pearls I inherited from you, I treasure the intangible "pearls" more.

I know the pearls with which you adorned me—by heart! One such pearl is that no matter where I'm going or what I'm doing, I'm always to remember who I am. Knowing who I am gives me confidence. This confidence eliminates "turf" wars, intimidation, and unfair com-parisons. Far from arrogance, this confidence is the absolute assurance that I know who I am, where I begin, and where I end. Grasping a position, whether rightfully mine or not, is simply not an option. I especially appreciate the freedom from threats that comes with this pearl. Its value is also enhanced because your mother gave it to you; you treasured it and passed it down to me.

Another pearl is the necessity of being involved in something greater than myself. Life is more fun, focused, and fulfilled when I can rise above the mediocrity of my own parameters and glimpse greater reality. It is then that I remember that troubles cannot defeat me as long as I am involved beyond myself—usually with other people.

One pearl that I hated for years is Romans 8:28, "And we know that in all things God works for the good of those who love him, who have been called according to his purpose." The day I hated it the most was the day when we were on our way to White Lake, had trouble with the car, and had to return home. You quoted that Scripture and seemed so sure that it was true. I was furious, disappointed, and convinced that you were demented. Much later I came to appreciate both the Scripture and the way you applied it to your life. As a mother and grandmother myself, I hope that I can exemplify my assurance to my loved ones that God himself is at work in our lives in both the good and the bad events. He is orchestrating masterpieces which are clear to him, but not always clear to us.

Another pearl on my string, is giving others something tangible. Counsel and love and time are good, but sometimes people feel better receiving something they can see, touch, or taste! We lived within our limited budget, but I saw you give a teenager or a young mother a dollar (quite a lot in the fifties) just so they'd have a little money of their own. More often, I saw you give flowers you had cut and arranged yourself, homemade cakes, clothes, vegetables from our garden, bookmarks, and Bibles. Because of your example, I have had a candy jar in my office for over fifteen years to share with my students. This "giving pearl" was also a legacy to you from your mother. I hope to pass these heirlooms on to my daughter.

Some more of the pearls in my character, add-a-pearl necklace, are these: maintaining a strong work ethic, encouraging disheartened people, remembering the advantages when they are hiding behind the disadvantages, laughing at myself so that others can laugh with me and not at me, choosing not to whine when whining would feel so gratifying, allowing others to be real even when I am not especially comfortable with their "realness," and understanding that spiritual excellence is a continuing process.

Choosing which pearls to include in this epistle is not easy. Certain "pearls of great price," however, cannot be excluded. The kind of marriage you and Daddy had and lived is priceless. I had such a wonderful home life with parents who had a truly great relationship. The second great price pearl is similar. When you came to visit us during our marriage, you always told me to let my husband Joe know every day how much I appreciated him. You were a widow, and I thought you were just missing Daddy, but I listened. Despite my many imperfections, I do not take my husband for granted. He knows that I know how wonderful he is and that I'd be lost without him. You helped me make that intentional effort, and I am forever grateful.

It's been over two years now since you passed on to an even greater life. I miss you so much at times that the pain seems physically unbearable. When that happens, I can almost hear you say, "Don't be sad that I'm gone; be thankful for the time we had." As you know, you said those words to me at airports many times when we were saying our goodbyes.

I'm so proud that you were my mother. An ordained minister for over sixty years—wow. You continued to study and learn and adapt in order to reach and understand others. At eighty-five, you still taught a large Sunday School class, led intercessory prayer groups, and held a staff position at a huge church. You often said that because of "backsliding" as a child and teenager, you wondered in your early Christian life if you could ever be faithful. That admission helped many a young person—especially me—believe that faithfulness really was possible. I'm certain that you've heard it from the Lord already, but I just want to let you know that you finished well—very well, indeed.

With love, honor, and longing,

Your only daughter, Char

Listen, my son,

to your father's instruction
and do not forsake your mother's teaching.
They will be a garland to grace your head
and a chain to adorn your neck.

Proverbs 1:8–9

The kingdom of heaven is like a
merchant looking for fine pearls. When he
found one of great value, he went away and sold
everything he had and bought it.

Matthew 13:45–46

Gold there is, and rubies in abundance,
but lips that speak knowledge are a rare jewel.

Proverbs 20:15

Imagination is the Mother of Invention

I come from a family blessed with creative gifts, and my mother's wonderful gift of creativity was evidenced in virtually every area of my childhood. One of my most frequent and enduring memories is of her bent over her sewing machine hour after hour. She sewed most of the clothes that my sister Brenda and I wore. To be honest, we didn't appreciate her sewing skills very much at the time, especially when she called us in from a great game of hide-and-go-seek to stand still for fifteen minutes while she fit a pair of pants or a dress she was working on. I learned to stand very, very still, even as hyperactive as I was, or I paid the price in pinpricks!

She made us the most incredible Barbie clothes as well. Sometimes she would buy remnants of tulle and glamorous fabrics to make ball gowns. Other times she utilized scraps from our own dresses to make matching outfits for our dolls.

I was so proud to carry my Barbie in her matching dress to church or to a friend's house.

I never appreciated her patience and love more than when I, as a young mother tried to duplicate her feats for my own daughters. I discovered that sewing Barbie clothes requires every bit the skill of normal sewing and more so—for smaller in this case definitely does not mean easier!

My parents had a continual struggle financially, but because of my mother's resourcefulness I cannot ever remember feeling poor. Sometimes on Saturday, my father would make a trip to the dump. My mother was usually a little apprehensive about letting him go, for she never quite knew what he would drag home. He loved to scavenge around finding things they could transform together from trash to treasure. She often chastised him for bringing home more things than he threw away!

Because of my mother's resourcefulness I cannot ever remember feeling poor.

One trip was particularly successful. My father brought home a complete child's play kitchen set. My parents meticulously cleaned and restored it, making new knobs and replacing worn decorations until it was better than new. Brenda and I played in that kitchen every day for many years.

When I became a mother and decided to stay home with my girls, we too struggled to make ends meet. Yet I never worried that my children would feel deprived. Instead I followed my mother's example and scoured garage sales to find clothes and toys I could reclaim for them.

In my childhood, we often made trips to thrift stores, where my mom would search for old dresses and accessories for our dress-up box. Some items she would remake, adding sparkling trims or lace to make them more special. Others she merely cleaned and shortened to make them fit our diminutive statures. Everyone wanted to play at our house where we had everything we needed to put on a play or practice being mommies to our dollies.

Everyone wanted to play at our house.

When my girls were growing up I followed my mom's lead and created a dress-up box for them. The best finds from garage sales, thrift shops and hand-me-downs went into their dress-up chest. I discovered a terrific factory outlet store where I often found brand new evening gowns in size 3 or 4 for under $20—less than the price of most new toys with many times the hours of use!

Mom also taught us her skills, frequently over our loud, childish protests! She not only taught us to sew, but required us to sew half of our school wardrobe in high school. We weren't easy to teach and it took a great amount of time away from things she could have been doing for herself, yet the skills we learned from sewing had a greater application than even she imagined. We learned to read and follow directions, we learned that big jobs can be accomplished in many small steps, we learned that each skill you gain makes the next achievement easier to accomplish and we learned a special kind of confidence that only comes from mastery. My mother's goals of producing competence had a side-benefit of building into us a self-esteem that we now realize cannot be produced in any other way.

Thank you, Mom, for your training and example.

Thank you, Mom. Because of your training and example, when I became a young mother and was equally financially challenged, I knew that with an ounce of imagination and an eye for a bargain I too could transform trash into treasure. I could use my creative talents to express my love and to make my own children have as rich a childhood as I had.

Mom

One of
the most
priceless
gifts
you ever
gave me
was
your time.

*From the fruit of his lips a man is
filled with good things
as surely as the work of his hands
rewards him.*

Proverbs 12:14

*Do you see a man skilled in his work?
He will serve before kings;
he will not serve before obscure men.*

Proverbs 22:29

*Skill will bring
success.*

Ecclesiastes 10:10

Thank you, Mom, for all you've done to give me life and for teaching me how to live it! I love you.

Recently, after having spent a week apart traveling to yet another city and yet another trade show, our family decided to go out to dinner to do some catching up. As we settled in and began looking over the menu, I noticed an intriguing family at a long table across from us.

Ten people were arranged around the table like zigzagging stair-steps. It took me a moment to realize that this was a single family and not a birthday party! The mother was at one end with a two-year old on her lap and the father sat at "three o'clock" with a six-month old daughter in his arms. Several small children were sandwiched in between and around them, their eyes riveted on their parents. All eight children were girls. Each set of eyes sparkled and their meal was accompanied by the tinkling sounds of muted laughter punctuated by boisterous giggles.

The two oldest girls sat at the far end of the rectangle. Sometimes they talked with each other; sometimes they reached over to help a younger sister with her dinner. The patience and love of the mother was fully reflected and modeled in the older sisters' gentle care of their younger sisters.

These children felt fully secure in their mother's love

I was fascinated and intrigued by this family of eight children; they were polite, well-mannered, and yet delightfully childlike. They made up games, talked with each other, and responded to their parents' instructions. One little girl even entertained herself off and on by playing with a salt shaker.

The mother had such a quiet spirit about her. She alternately held first one child and then another, and each waited patiently for her turn in her arms. It was obvious that these children felt fully secure in their mother's love for them and were not jealous of the attention paid to the others.

As I thought about these things, my mind wandered back a few years to my grandparents' sixty-fifth wedding anniversary. Our family had gathered together from all across the country to celebrate my grandparents' love and legacy. Each of my five aunts, my father, and various grandchildren took turns telling stories of the things they remembered about their growing-up years. They talked of the impact my grandparents' marriage had on them, and especially my grandmother's love for each of them.

We shed rivers of tears. Many times a speaker had to pause to gain composure, unable to proceed until the lump in his or her throat melted away.

One theme soared above all the others ... *"I always felt important to you, Mom.* No matter how busy you were, you made it seem like you had all the time in the world to listen to me."* Raising six children involved many overwhelming and unavoidable daily tasks, yet in the midst of it all, my grandmother had been able to make each child feel profoundly and completely loved. I was amazed that not one of my aunts' stories involved anything particularly heroic or unusual. It had been in the small, everyday things that Grandmother blessed her children the most—things like stopping a household chore to listen to a silly joke, reading Bible stories and teaching them about God, or taking a moment to pray over a pressing need. She had "slumber parties" where she would stay up late at night and talk with her girls, asking insightful questions and encouraging them. It was these little things that my grandmother did—just like the mother in the restaurant was doing with her children—that made my father and aunts feel so wonderfully secure.

Her children rose up to call her blessed

At the end of the anniversary celebration, my grandmother was speechless—a highly unusual occurrence! She had been emotionally overwhelmed with the outpouring of affection and encouragement as "her children rose up to call her blessed."

My attention was drawn back to the family of ten across from us. I had a pretty good idea that this family wasn't always so well-ordered and perfectly mannered. Surely they had their moments of frustration and anguish, angst and exhaustion. How many days did this mother wonder if she was doing anything important in life? Did her extended family support her in her commitment to make the world a better place by raising an abundance of well-nurtured children?

I saw her great worth reflected in the adoring eyes of her children

I wondered if this momentarily serene mother of eight realized the richness of her inheritance. I saw her great worth so clearly reflected in the attentive and adoring eyes of her children. She was as royal as a queen and was as highly revered. But did she *feel valued and valuable*? Do you?

I wish I could carry you both away to a day somewhere in your distant future when your families, too, will be gathered around you both, honoring you with their words and with their hearts.

I talked with this mother after their meal and discovered that she was home-schooling her girls. Their family had chosen to make sacrifices in lifestyle that allowed her to invest her life in teaching her children. She had chosen to devote this season of her life to shaping the next generation.

Not every mother is called to raise eight children and home school them, but every mother's call is an important one. When you have devoted yourself to the lofty calling of shaping the next generation, your treasure will never rust or mildew, and it won't rot away or gather dust like an award on a shelf. Perhaps neither you nor this mother I met in the restaurant will ever stand upon a platform and receive an award publicly acknowledging your efforts as a mother. But your living rewards will only continue to grow and gain in value.

Mother Listened

By Dawn Anspaugh

My mother was the "listening ear" of our family and our community. I remember her standing with her ear to the phone for long periods of time listening to anyone in our community who phoned in time of trouble. I used to marvel at the number of people who would phone when they were in distress, even those who would not normally call just to chitchat.

Mother had no training in counseling and, in fact, seldom gave advice. Instead she would simply utter empathetic syllables to assure the caller that she was listening and caring. The callers sought her out as someone who would care, listen attentively, and help carry their burdens. Perhaps even the unsaved could sense that she would "carry their burdens to the Lord in prayer." Even though we three daughters had to share her with the community and extended family, we knew we could have that same "listening ear" whenever we needed it.

Now That I'm a Mother

By Londa Alderink

I wonder if every woman's relationship with her mother changes when she has a baby. Mine certainly did! My mom and I have not always seen eye-to-eye. In fact, we've clashed a lot through the years. That didn't necessarily change when my daughter was born—what did change is my heart for my mom. I've always loved her dearly, but I wondered many times if I would ever understand her.

Growing up, I always thought she was too strict. But now that I have my own child, I know in my heart that she was doing her best to keep me safe and protected. When I was younger, I also thought she expected too much of me. But now I know that she only wanted me to give my all in everything because she knew things in life worth having never come easy.

I also couldn't understand why she talked about God all the time—after all, I believed in him. But now I understand that she wanted me to intimately know and love the One who gives life, both physically and eternally—the One who will always watch over me no matter how far I wander.

Yes, now that I have my own child I finally understand my mom—just like she always told me I would. And even though she told me many times how much I mean to her, I finally really know how much, because I know how much my own daughter means to me. I understand my mom because now, I'm one, too.

Lord, thank you for blessing me with a mother who emulated you in so many ways—patient, caring, abounding in love. And thank you for giving me a genuine understanding of my mom and a deepening love for her. I pray that one day my daughter will understand me in the same way. Amen.

The endless circle of
a
Mother's
love

Nurturing & caring ... helpful & kind ... teaching ... soothing ... sharing laughter & tears ... giving ...

©1997 Audrey Jeanne Roberts   Author/Artist 389

You will increase my honor
and comfort me once again, O Lord.

Psalm 71:21

"*Honor your father and mother*"

—which is the first commandment with a promise—
"that it may go well with you and that you may
enjoy long life on the earth."

Ephesians 6:2

"Then the King will say to those on his right, 'Come, you who are blessed by my Father; take your inheritance, the kingdom prepared for you since the creation of the world. For I was hungry and you gave me something to eat, I was thirsty and you gave me something to drink, I was a stranger and you invited me in, I needed clothes and you clothed me, I was sick and you looked after me, I was in prison and you came to visit me.'

"Then the righteous will answer him, 'Lord, when did we see you hungry and feed you, or thirsty and give you something to drink? When did we see you a stranger and invite you in, or needing clothes and clothe you? When did we see you sick or in prison and go to visit you?'

"The King will reply, 'I tell you the truth, whatever you did for one of the least of these brothers of mine, you did for me.'"

Matthew 25:34–40

Sources

Carson, Ben with Gregg Lewis. *The Big Picture.* © 1999
by Benjamin Carson. Grand Rapids, Michigan:
Zondervan, 1999.

Tada, Joni Eareckson. *More Precious Than Silver.*
© 1998 by Joni Eareckson Tada. Grand Rapids,
Michigan: Zondervan, 1998.

Weems, Ann, retold by Alice Gray. "Heirloom." *More
Stories for the Heart.* © 1997 by Multnomah
Publishers, Inc. Originally quoted in *Parables, Etc.*,
December 1986. Sisters, Oregon: Multnomah
Publishers, Inc., 1997.

Special thanks to Amy E. Langeler, Linda Fode, Jessica
Start, Molly C. Detweiler, Sallylou Dotson, Char
Iaquinta, Dawn Anspaugh, and Londa Alderink
for sharing their tributes.